The Debt Solution
By: Genne L. Pangelinan

Disclaimer Notice

While all attempts have been made to ensure the information provided in this book, the author does not assume/claim any responsibility for errors, omissions, or contrary interpretations of the subject matter contained within. The information provided in this book is for educational and entertainment purposes only. The reader is responsible for his/her own actions and the author does not and will not accept any responsibilities for any liabilities or damages, real or perceived, resulting from the use of this information.

Print Book May Be A Little Different From The Electronic Version, Also Known As Ebooks.

Table Of Contents

Introduction	4
What Is A Budget?	5
Why Many Fail In Budgeting?	7
The Big Debt Solution	8
Chart #1 (Debt Solution Example)	15
Chart #2 (Debt Solution Example)	21
Simple Savings Tips	22

Introduction

Are you deeply into debt? Are your bills piling up, struggling to keep up with payments?

Well, fortunately you found this book. This is your stepping stone to restore financial balance back into your life! Yes, I am talking about paying off debts, avoiding the road to bankruptcy without changing your lifestyle. Make the most of your money with tips of purchasing things. That is the mission i gave this book. Sounds insane? It does, but not impossible. All it takes is just a simple word, "COMMITMENT". This simple commitment you are about to enter is probably the most important commitment in your life. Remember all these steps are the key points to your success.

What Is A Budget?

It's simply a fix amount of expenditure for a set amount of time.

Why Having A Budget Is Important
- Having a budget tends to keep you focused on the goal.
- This will helps avoid spending money you do not own such as "credit cards".
- Strong budgeting can lead you to a bigger, better retirement.
- Financially prepared for any emergencies.
- Helps you identify those impulsive spending habits.
- Less stress to worry about after the budgeting plan is set in motion.

Why Many Fail In Budgeting?

- The budget you have set may have been too restrictive. No room for some play with a budget.
- Goal(s) were not set. Improves motivation by focusing on a concrete goal.
- No support. Sometimes no support can bog you down and you will lose concentration.
- Emergency plans were not created. You were not ready for any emergencies.
- Time was not on your side. The time you have given yourself may have not been too realistic, or not enough wiggle room within the budget.
- Frustration. This usually occurs when you see no progression within your personal finance.

The Big Debt Solution

Step 1: Understanding Debt

We all know what debt is, meaning you owe a lender money. Debt Itself can cause emotional stress, broken homes, and even suicide to some victims. It attacks you when you are most vulnerable. The buy now and pay later concept has swallowed up many lives. For example, you desperately want to purchase the most up to date phone, but you don't have the money. So, you use a credit card because desperate times calls for desperate measures. Now you owe a couple hundred bucks to your lender.

As days pass by, you feel comfortable swiping your credit card, buying things without any cash on hand, this is called impulsive buying behavior. This is the number one thing you must overcome. Stores are well designed to accommodate those urges of impulsive buying behavior. Have you ever noticed that the most important stuff you need are usually in the way back of most stores. Think of it this way, you go to Walmart or Kmart to buy laundry detergent and the first thing you see are the sale signs. You walk past a couple isles and noticed some snacks that are on sale and start to fill up your cart or basket before getting to the item you really came for. So, instead of less than $10 worth of merchandise, you bought $30 worth. It happens to everyone impulsive buying behavior leads to debt.

Lets say, now you owe a couple thousand dollars and the billing cycle starts. Lenders do not care about the amount of money you spend. It is the interest rates that they pay most attention to. Lenders make their income through interest rates. So, the more money you owe, the longer it takes to pay off your debt. The longer you owe money, the more lenders make off you. Have you ever noticed that every time you pay your monthly credit card bill, it comes back to your available balance. Does it make sense now, why lenders want to keep you in their debt game, wanting to squeeze as much money from you as possible.

Lets say you cannot pay your credit card bills or loans. Now, you are on the verge of getting your assets taken from you because you failed to pay. This is what you would want to avoid. This can lead to emotional stress, broken homes, and maybe even suicide depending on what factors come into play. Most people are lead to a popular remedy for this situation is filing bankruptcy. Yes, bankruptcy may help, but not entirely. It can also hurt you in some ways, such as destroying your name with credit reports. You will have a hard time getting approved for another loan within a 7-10 year radius. Some employers will ask you if you ever filed for bankruptcy. Remember debt will always hurt you one way or another.

Step 2: Commitment
To start off with your new approach of debt relief, you must make a commitment. You must keep in mind that debt is only a phase in life. You have only two options to get out of this phase. The easy way or the hard way. Most people choose the easy way out. That is the reason I wrote this book.
Sometimes the easy way out is not always the easy way out of situations like yours.

Let us talk about the hard way out. It can take a little time and effort, but it comes with the biggest reward. Think about it, getting rid of debts easy with this strategy. This is the most simple method and probably the cheapest. You do not need to file for anything, go to court, or any other obstacles that may get in your way. I know it sounds ridiculous, but it is not.

Now, the big commitment. You must be serious about your situation. Look at yourself in the mirror and say "I AM GETTING OUT OF DEBT". Tell your spouse, your kids, friends, and family that you are getting out of debt. This is where it gets psychological, when you let people or even someone important in your life know what you intend to do, you wouldn't want to let them down. So, your only option is to follow through with your word or commitment. You can also use this strategy for future use.

Chart #1 (Debt Solution Example)
Step 3: Organization

After your big commitment, it takes preparation and organization to bail yourself out of debt. Gather all your Loans (Home loan, Auto loan, and Personal loan) and credit card bills. You are gonna need to write on a sheet of paper or you may use Microsoft spreadsheet .Organize them from least to greatest on the amount you owe. Basically creating a list of your debts. Most bills are paid monthly. Next, calculate all your income you make a month. With all your debts gathered in one place, it should look like this:

Debt Description	Debt Amount	Monthly Bill Amount	Due Date	Extra Payments
Credit Card #1	$1,500	$45	7th of every month	
Credit Card #2	$6,000	$180	7th of every month	
Auto Loan	$25,000	$360	10th of every month	
Home Loan	$150,000	$625	10th of every month	

Step 4: The Snowball Effect

Now, I am going to show you a secret weapon in the financial world. It is called the "Snowball Effect". You will see your debts decrease month after month until you are debt free. If you take a good look at the table from the previous page, you will notice that the Extra Payments column is blank. That is Where the Snowball Effect comes into play.

The only amount you need to invest is $20 every month. Yes, that $20 bill you are about to invest is the starting point of the Snowball Effect. This strategy requires you to focus your extra payments on one bill at a time. The other bills are to be paid at its minimum until it is that bill's turn to be eliminated. Back to your debt sheet, add that $20 bill to your payments every month with credit card #1. You will understand that you do not need to change your lifestyle because of debt. Keep that extra payment every month until credit card #1 is payed off.

It gets more interesting the longer you play this game against debt. After Credit Card #1 is payed off, add its monthly payments to your next target. The next target on the list is Credit Card #2. So, the monthly payment jumps from $180.00 to $225.00 because $45.00 + $180.00 = $225.00. That is an additional payment of $45. Are you starting to see the Snowball Effect, it is eliminating the debt of credit card #2.

Now Auto Loan is the next target. Use the same exact method you used on Credit Card #2. Add the $225.00 to the monthly Auto Loan payments. Now it jumps from $360.00 to $585.00 because $45.00 + $180.00 + $360.00 = $585.00. Look at the table on the next page to help understand more.

Side Note: *Use The Chart(s) To Guide You Through Your Debt Management Crisis.*

See Chart On The Next Page

Chart #2 (Debt Solution Example)

Debt Description	Debt Amount	Monthly Bill Amount	Due Date	Extra Payments
Credit Card #1	$1,500	$45	7th of every month	$20
Credit Card #2	$6,000	$180	7th of every month	None
Auto Loan	$25,000	$360	10th of every month	None
Home Loan	$150,000	$625	10th of every month	None

Simple Savings Tips

- Sign up for rewards programs from businesses
- Write a list before you go shopping and stick to it
- Cut back on convenient foods such as fast food restaurants and microwavables
- Shop at the local market where everything is fresh
- Try out some generic brands on items you use regularly
- Start a vegetable garden
- Air seal your home to spend less on the electric bill
- Cancel the cable channels you don't watch
- Use a fuel efficient car
- Turn off the air conditioner in your car
- Cancel Proprietary credit cards
- Use long distance calls off the internet, such as skype and other apps
- Go shopping with discount coupons
- Buy your flight ticket at travelocity.com or other websites that offer great rates
- Take advantage of loss leaders at your local stores
- Ebay can offer many cheap stuff with potential savings

As you can see, the hard way is always the most rewarding. Now you are ready to conquer your consumer debt.

Hopefully this makes a big impact to you and others as well. Thank You And Good Luck!!!

Sincerely,
Genne L. Pangelinan

This Book Is Also Available On Amazon Kindle!

You Can Grab A Copy At Amazon.com

www.ingramcontent.com/pod-product-compliance
Lightning Source LLC
Chambersburg PA
CBHW070721210526
45170CB00021B/1398